The **AMBULANCE** Service

Contents

999 Emergency   2

Accident and Emergency   4

Different Types of Help   6

Cars and Motorbikes   8

The Air Ambulance   10

Back to School   12

How You Can Help the Ambulance Service   14

Glossary   16

Index   16

Monica Hughes

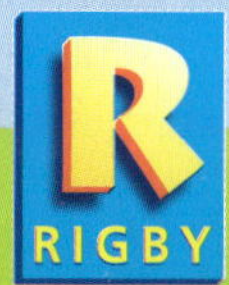

999 Emergency

John calls 999. It is an emergency. His mother has had an accident.

An ambulance is
sent out.

The ambulance crew
will help John's mother
and then take her
to hospital.

*The ambulance
control centre.*

ACCIDENT and Emergency

An ambulance is often sent to help at an accident on the road or the railway. The ambulance crew work with the police and firefighters at many accidents.

People who have been injured are taken to hospital in the ambulance.

Different Types of **HELP**

The Ambulance Service does not only help in accidents and emergencies. Ambulances are used every day to take people to and from hospital appointments, to **clinics** and **day centres**.

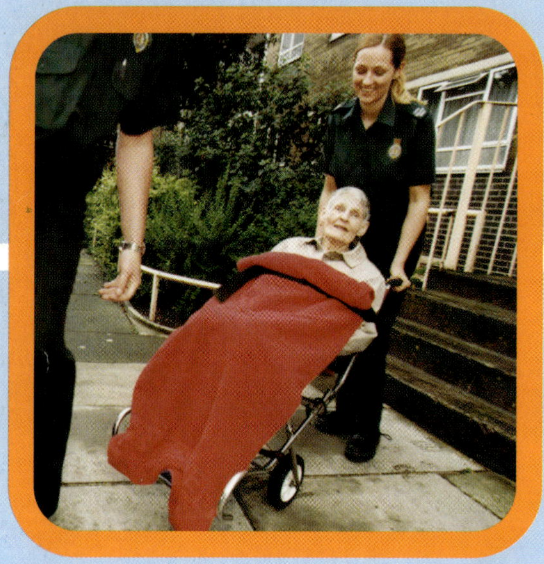

Transport ambulance crews help people to and from the ambulance.

A transport ambulance is like a minibus and can carry several people.

CARS and Motorbikes

The Ambulance Service sometimes sends cars or motorbikes to accidents and emergencies. A **paramedic** in a car can help a patient and also take them to hospital.

Paramedics are soon on the scene to help the patient and police.

A paramedic on a motorbike can get through traffic very quickly. He or she helps the patient until an ambulance arrives.

The Air **AMBULANCE**

The Air Ambulance can reach places that a road ambulance can't. It can also get to places very quickly. Sometime the Air Ambulance is the quickest and only way to get a patient to hospital.

Air Ambulances can reach difficult places, such as cliff tops, beaches, or countryside where there are no roads.

The Air Ambulance paramedics carry the patient by stretcher to the Air Ambulance.

Many Air Ambulances are run by money from **charities** and companies.

BACK to School

There is a lot to learn in the Ambulance Service. Some people learn about working in the control centre. Other people learn how to drive an ambulance.

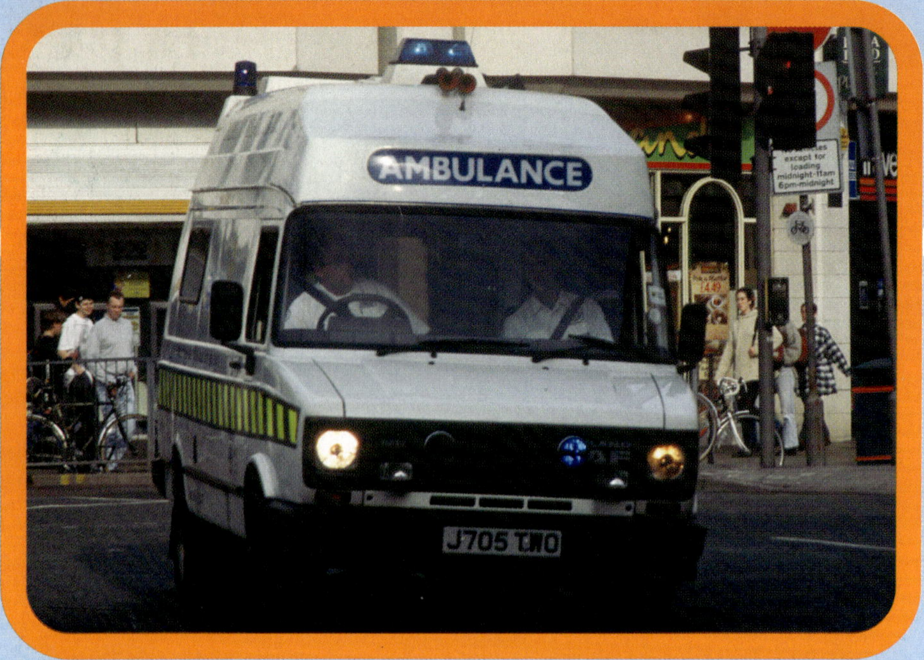

It can take many months to learn how to drive an ambulance quickly and safely.

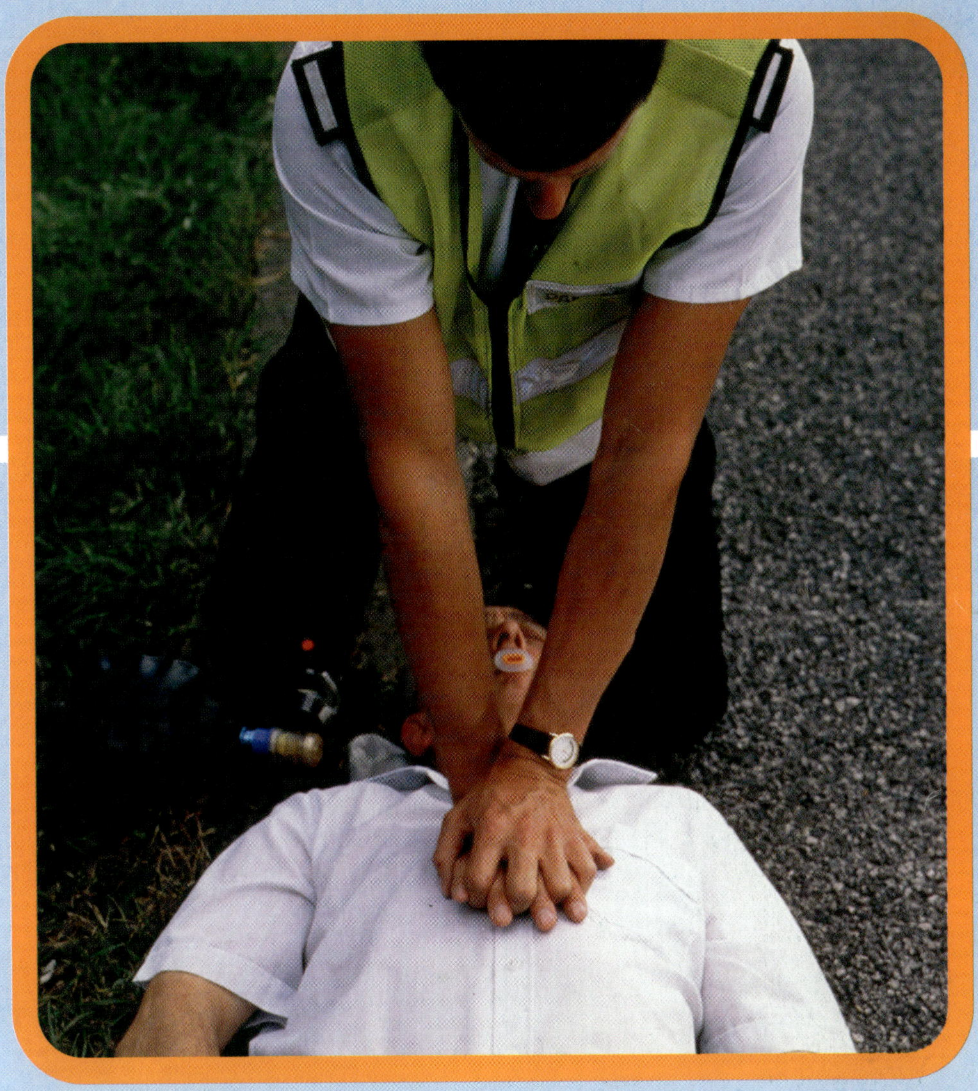

The paramedics learn about different kinds of **treatment**. They also learn how to use different kinds of **equipment**.

HOW You Can Help the Ambulance Service

- Move out of the way if you see an ambulance with its lights flashing, or you hear its **siren** sounding.

- Make sure you know your address and that it is easy for an ambulance to find your home, even in the dark.

- Make a collection to support your local Air Ambulance.

Glossary

charities organisations that help people

clinic places where people are given treatment

day centre places where people go to be cared for
  in the day

equipment tools that people use to do special jobs

paramedic a member of the ambulance crew that
  is trained to treat patients

treatment medicine or care people are given
  when injured or sick

siren part of an ambulance that makes a loud noise

Index

accident 2, 4, 6, 8

ambulance 3, 4-5, 6-7, 8-9, 10-11, 12, 14-15

emergency 2, 6, 8

hospital 3, 5, 6, 8, 10

paramedic 8-9, 13